*

**

Maple Leaf Rag VI

B/W reproduction of a painting of the Maple Leaf Bar
on Oak Street by Michael S. True.

Intro note

It's doubtful that anyone back in 1979 would have thought the weekly poetry readings at the Maple Leaf Bar would continue on for so long. That's one reason why we have compiled this 6th edition of the *Maple Leaf Rag* anthology: To honor those who have shared their poetic verses on Sunday afternoons out on the back patio of the renowned New Orleans music club (8316 Oak Street).

In a city known more for celebrating musicians, visual artists, actors and chefs, some might wonder how a poetry reading series could last for decades. Well, first, special thanks must go to Hank Staples, proprietor of the Maple Leaf, and to host Nancy Harris. Hank was a good friend of poet Everette Maddox, one of the founders of those first readings, and he has seen the value and need for the venue. Second, Nancy has dedicated herself to encouraging poets, week after week, through good times (Mardi Gras & book publications) and bad (9/11 and war & Hurricane Katrina), for more than 25 years. "It's almost like going to church, a church of poetry," Harris has said.

As might be expected, some of the participants, including the founders, have passed on. Everette Maddox died in 1989 after hosting the readings for 10 years. See the tribute to Everette by singer/songwriter Les Kerr, especially his song "Inspiration & Bar Scotch" on page 56. Poet Maxine Cassin, publisher of the first *Maple Leaf Rag*, died in 2010.

If one does the math, approximately 50,000 poems have probably been shared at The Maple Leaf over the life span of the readings. (50 weeks X 10 poets X 3 poems each X 38 years = ??).

Prize-winning poet BJ Ward of New Jersey, a recent reader, had this to say about the Maple Leaf: "As I said (during the reading), the Maple Leaf is the best bar poetry scene in the nation (followed closely—but not surpassed—by Bar 13 in Manhattan and the Jackson Inn in Wilmington, Delaware).

Anyway, herein is a sampling of some of the poetic writings that have been presented by both local and out-of-town writers. Here's hoping readers will connect with some of the poems and that, as Everette used to say, "Umpteen" more will be created and shared in the future!

-- JP Travis

*

Maple Leaf Rag VI

An anthology of poetic writings
New Orleans, Louisiana

Cover image is a reproduction of a painting titled "Celebration of Spirits" by Randy "Frenchy" Frechette.
© by *Frenchy*   frenchylive.com

Frontispiece (p. 3). Reproduction of a painting of the Maple Leaf Bar by Michael S. True.

Photographs by Edgar Sierra, JP Travis & Nancy Harris.

Grateful acknowledgements: Some of the works in this anthology have appeared in other publicaions, including the following:

"Dirty Blues" by Rodney Jones was first published in *Things That Happened Once* and later in *Salvation Blues* (both by Houghton Mifflin).

"Ode to the Middle Finger" by BJ Ward was originally published in *American Poetry Review* and later, along with "And All the Peasants Cheered for the King. The End," published in *Jackleg Opera: Collected Poems, 1990 to 2013* by North Atlantic Books.

Published by Portals Press
New Orleans, Louisiana USA
www.portalspress.com

ISBN 978-0-9970666-1-6

Table of Contents

Contents

Contents

Ralph Adamo

Pre-Sleep

It is threatening to rain, we say,
a classic case of when an antecedent
would come in handy, and why
such a threat should be leveled
at innocents like us – well, it
is the innocent who suffer, isn't
it? more than the ones with
ridges and grooves

Ambition, desire, need –
let's pull them apart, like muscles
that have pathologically entwined and head

for the dreamscape of the day before

or maybe just bed, where after a while
the things we see with our eyes closed – the open eyes,
the clenched face, the crowd growing aerially smaller, a
point so lit the closed eye burns with it, then fear, then
grief, until at last the human beast gives out and sleep
arrives like an old body putting one foot forward to stumble
against all the years piled atop the river running blue

---uncompromising old age, storm unto death ---

how ordinary we survivors seem
claiming the earth's surface, accepting the sun as given...

Ralph Adamo

This Is Now

Mine is sensual and forlorn,
Jones all humanist and half divine,
Leon so angry through spitting laughter,
Sam sad, born to look away, eyeballs
like gritted teeth, and Stoss -- luxuriant
lover exhaled by long-departed deities...
the women I did not understand as they
have understood since first light, nor
the singing man still standing knife deep in
his heart that cannot bleed. We spoke
on mountaintops, it's true, low mountains,
but more in late-night diners, and cars
unfit for the road, declaring too on porches,
the smoky room, yards only nature kept.
One of us missed those early end times,
these memories, honorary, aloof, untrue,
but should've been there, not half so
lost as we few in that day, scared to the
breaking point, closing in on it.
We could have used the cloth, some
honeyed breathing, and the rest.

Robert Allen

Two Haiku

Warriors kill
The dragon
They become

    *****

World peace
Dogs of war
Just sleeping

Tim Andersen

What the Hell

Dad came home and noticed I was wearing
my Knights of Columbus t-shirt so he asked me
how I did and I told him I struck out four times
and he said "What the hell kind of deal is that?
Striking out four times?" Then he told me he
would take me to a Twins game if I got a hit
the next game. So I got a hit the next game
and one Saturday we all piled into the '63 gold
Rambler wagon and dad yelled all the way to
Minneapolis and once inside Gates Brown hit a
batting practice homer right to me but it went
through my hands -- I should have brought my
mitt -- so the whole family yells, "What the hell
kind of deal is that? It was right to you."

After the game, we hung out for autographs
and Tony Oliva, looking dapper in a summer
suit and Panama hat, emerged from the clubhouse
and signed a hundred autographs but not ours
so dad yells "What the hell kind of deal is that?
We pay your inflated salary." But Tony Oliva
took no nevermind out to his car. Then we drove
to McDonald's where we ordered ten large fries
with extra salt with our burgers and root beer
and luckily the Rambler had four circular indentations
on the inside of the glove compartment door
which helped us out a lot because it gave us
someplace to set our drinks whenever we dined
in our car which was often and it was quiet in the
car while we ate so that was my favorite family activity

Katy Balma

The Fountain of Relative Age

You dip in, become who you are.

A fun-loving fitness coach finally resembles
the twelve-year-old boy he emits.
His cannonballs punctuate bold yippees.

A third grade belle in terrycloth wrap, flush
with spelling bee medals, emerges a ripe twenty-two.
The neighborhood sociopath truncates
to toddler. He steps out of his blue
uniform and wails, confused. Responsibilities,

rights and roles reassigned
according to each new body, the world adjusts!

Except for those who don't change, who swim for hours
unaffected. These get out, dry off, scarf down
their tuna salad sandwich halves, their Gala apple slices,
wondering why everyone took off.

Katy Balma

Lingua Franca

There's a language I understand but barely speak.
What I can say in that language I say
with near-native vowels and intonations, but I never get
past present tense. I can say, "This is my husband,
my family," not, "This was my husband, my family,"
nor, "This will be my husband, my family." I cannot say, even,
"This was / will be my life." Mother says I am stuck
in the past, because I would continue a marriage
with the language I began for love
of a man who left. (I can't say, "He left me." I can say,
"I'm abandoned.") but she and I only use English,
and it's clear that I lack the grammatical range
to be anything but a Buddhist in the tongue
of the man I married. Plus, I can use adjectives:
"This is my former husband. This is my old life,
my new life." I could even say, "This is my child"—a future
sentence parsed in present tense, the past written all over it.

Grace Bauer

REVENANT

It was the walk -- half amble, half swagger –
that took me back thirty years to an ordinary morning
on St. Charles, waiting for the streetcar to rattle
me to work and watching from the neutral ground
as you headed into the K & B -- and my heart, I swear,
it swelled – a feeling so visceral I imagined
some passerby might see it rising above me
into the live oaks that lined the avenue --
like in those old cartoons where Krazy Kat
gazed at Ignatz, her unrequited longing
an untethered balloon bound, of course, to burst.
I smiled (we're back in today now) at the guy
walking towards me. He nodded. His eyes nowhere
near as blue as yours. And you, my love, remained dead,
even as I turned to watch you – back in my world
for that instant -- and walking, again, away.

Steve Beisner

Time and Space

With apologies to A. Einstein.

the crawfish swims backwards when his world is disturbed
pushing through muddy water tail first towards what he can
not see

he faces his past, where he has been, not where he's going
moving through space, safer to be somewhere not here

yesterday, tomorrow, a moment from now are nothing.
now is all
move now

~ ~ ~

alone on a rainy morning
I'm strapped to a rail car
rushing down a narrow tunnel of time

unrelenting motion
hurrying forward in that single direction
towards an invisible future

how different is being caught in time
from the easy navigation through space

behind lie memories and life
ahead the unseen things to be

~ ~ ~

the crawfish has no regrets of his past
is never anxious for his future

who can say that swimming backwards

is not the perfect thing for this moment?

the crawfish backs into the fishers trap
is dumped into a boiling cauldron
is gone

life is poured out on a table
covered with old newspapers
devoured with cold beer and boiled corn

~ ~ ~

I stroll State Street crawfish-blind to my future
puzzling over time's one way arrow
and why the window glass between now and yet to be is opaque

two sidewalk blocks away
a man wears a yellow straw hat
a woman animates a short green skirt.

I exchange knowledge of space
for premonitions of future moments

in only minutes they will leave the future
walk into my present, fade into my past

if only I could see further down my road
by months, by years, by decades

but I know of no street that long
so I crawfish through life
seeing clearly only what is past
swimming in muddy water
forward through time
toward my unknowable end

Paul Benton

The Dog in the Boat

It was true, even if truth wasn't
the most important element,
true that there was a dog in a boat
rendered by someone's hand,
arranged and placed onto paper,
confined there and surrounded
by a simple black plastic frame —
a dog stands, forward-looking,
as it travels down a stream —
a multi-colored paisley body
of swirling water, pure
green trees and vegetation
line the banks. The dog's gaze
is set, eyes on fire with a distant sunrise,
sundown. What is the river's name?
The dog could not read those signs,
but each wave that kicked into
the side of the boat surely added
meaning and definition to the scene.

We would look at this picture
of the dog in the boat
and discuss the unknown future
as our sun rose and set
framed in that small room's
kitchen window, Vietnamese
voices spilling in from down the hall —
children playing games —
our words, our voices (sober or drunk)
navigated this limited space
day after day, and the dog in the boat
peered out steadfast into a point
behind us, beyond us,
illuminated by what was approaching.

Benton

Some days we would place the dog
in the boat away, there in the closet
as if testing our own philosophy,
but nothing really changed.
We carried on our conversations
in the quiet world, points being made,
then other ideas raised.
No, nothing was ever solved:
then we'd decide it was time
to bring back out the dog in the boat,
it was time we'd both agree.

What kind of dog was it?
It seemed to be all dogs,
the common dog with its
classic stance in the middle
of shifting terrain, fortified
by its dogness. We'd stand there
and drink the image in,
refreshed — this one canine,
eyes unblinking as it straddled
the rocking vessel, going somewhere.

Megan Burns

deadliest animals

/ other humans

poetry carts a wound to treasure light
random seduces, hard in glue. I soul throttled you.
we eat sentences/ what will you do for love
who can answer honestly
when our world breaks.   we break.   pour out
            till a scraping of bottom becomes

look how we terrible
dumb show is a wheel
we push to death

is there anything we won't do
to reach someone we miss
                    will you sit with me   while I channel

listen I trope
faltering/ he just disappeared
is it any better to be taken
out by hate
or by your own hand

dear art   I make of you
terror   so abundant
I'm drowning in this world
images pile on our fragile chests
                        holy, holy, holy eternity

Burns

we are all trapped

I could see into you   my love

and you broke

        my love

Voyager to Mother Earth

Tonight, almost three million miles from home,
I can imagine there are faces lighting up
as my eyes rove past this last Jovian planet
with its storms that will not end for centuries.
It is my final task to reveal to you
the eight moons of Neptune, zeroing in on Triton,
that contrary body to which I have been drawn
with its ice-ringed volcanoes and its methane
       atmosphere.

A constant stream of data translates to frozen
       stills
which you will study with great care from an earth
       that's scorched.
Will you hesitate one moment before you close my
       eyes
and send me beyond the sun deeper into space
where I must roam among the stars, blind as Oedipus?

Poet Christian Champagne, author of
Roach Opera and other works.

Dodd Clifton

THE ANCIENT PHILOSOPHY PROFESSOR

Some of my esteemed colleagues
Would perhaps think this a crackpot idea
But here it is
Imagine if you will a drug, an alchemical elixir
Of which there are several formulae
Each potion yielding the same pharmacological power
But they are different in appearance
In colour maybe, or perhaps viscosity
These are words in this analogy
In different languages
Written with the appropriate symbols
Each sounding foreign in their own way
But now the moment of truth
Each referring to the same idea
Or as close as a single concept
Can be captured and framed with letters
To be read by learned scholars
And pass over the lips
Of arcane sages and hermetic philosophers

Top: Storyteller Scott Edson. Bottom: Two poetry lovers from the Mississippi coast.

Marshall Deerfield

Two Haiku

Life sustained with words
poetry straight from the heart
the charm of soul food.

*****

Consciousness of heart
measured by a beating drum
earth calls to us all.

Marshall Deerfield

BUFFALO SOLIDARITY*

The buffalo appear
from nowhere
stampeding across
the prayerie
as they have
for millennia

They are the
life and blood
of ancestors

Our living relatives
cry out in solidarity

The white man
in riot gear
may not yet
know what
this means

But he will
once the buffalo
have again
swept across
this country
ending the tyranny
of the black snake
and restoring
life to its
proper balance.

*Buffalo Solidarity was written after watching livefeeds of the conflict at Standing Rock over the construction of the Dakota Access Pipeline, specifically on October 27, 2016, when hundreds of buffalo suddenly stampeded across the prairie.

Dean Ellis

BATTURE

April. A scrap of metal, remnant
of a long-sunken tug, coddles the
 riverbank, tangles with old fishing
line, adds ballast to the batture.
It rattles in the new breeze, a dogged
mortal on the river's undying flank.
Death as a sentinel against death,
life redeemed to its steadfast source.
College girls loll on the grass in
premature bikinis. A chill muffles
 the supine echo of summer; cracks
appear in the riverbed, rain is denied
 its reverie. Cities lay buried beneath
the oyster bed of winter, the seasons
are cantilevered. Time is moribund,
nothing occurs in stages. Each day
reaches inexorably into the next:
suddenly it rains, suddenly she
is gone, suddenly he is 50. A girl
smiles from the riverbank, evolution
is resurrected in all its imperfect glory.
The seasons know themselves again,
solitude settles into its hollow shoal,
a ripple of memory stirs
on the surface.
It is spring.

Gina Ferrara

Flying the Same

They stole my clothes
placed on the rocks, in my dreams
they plucked the figs, even the unripe,
they never brought notes or laurels,
often accompanied by couplets of magpies,
they wanted my eyes, ever widening,
each time I lost count of them
over Van Gogh's fields before harvest,
the gold stalks unscathed
by the machete, the crows appear
as hasty checks, incompletions,
scribbles, deep carvings, warnings
with slight arches, wings extended,
touching two directions
voluminous each time,
especially today flying toward a paler sky
the tall cypress nearly bare
in ways recognized.

Gina Ferrara

Swarm

Never one for an overnight genesis,
this act of creation takes time.
The bee keeper dispenses smoke
derived from burnt letters
and yesterday's news, the history
no one will question, a plume, a ribbon,
the sacred ashen sash that dissipates
before meeting any horizon.
In his suit, he looks ready to orbit,
to abandon the burdens of gravity
to leave the earth and its atrocities,
its wretched seasons.
Colorless and stiff, veiled, no knuckles
or ankles exposed, he sees odes of hexagons,
concentric configurations of purposeful combs,
and exaggerated commas, bees in a white wooden box--
the lid lifted, honey alleviating the bitterness
and the soft solidity of wax
offering an eventual arrival of light.

Poets Maria M. Kelson, Gina Ferrara & Melinda Palacio at a reading on the patio of the Maple Leaf in New Orleans.

Poet John Gery

John Gery

The End

They wait for it,
the only thing the young are patient for,
    as you mislead
yourself, certain that limp across the floor

you just limped wasn't
your knee's fault, but the floorboard's. You recall
    the time you ripped
clear through a glass door, shattering it all

to tiny pieces,
and walked away. You have no plans today
    but to complete
the seven hundred things you always say

you want to finish
before you die. It's easier to lie
    when in decline,
although for me that's one more reason why

the truth matters.
Your sudden urge to cry no one observes,
    yet older friends
envy the still sharp edges of your nerves

and sometimes curves
provide, fit in your soft palm, recompense,
    a moment's ease,
leased from the past. Some things make too much sense;

others defy
even madness as their cause. In the end
    no end seems right
nor sad, just something heavy every time you bend.

Mike Goetz

My Roots Grew Upside Down

My roots grew
upside down.
They started out
In space,
And it seems,
Each day, I
Stick my head,
Further and further,
Into the ground.
I really started
out with something,
And I'm afraid
It's gone.
Buried Underground.
I squandered
The best thing I
Could ever ask for.
My roots that grew
Upside down.
I saw Charon and
The Astral Belt.
But now I feel
That I have drowned.
A rotted fruit
From roots that grew
Upside down.
I can't remember
The last time I ever
Heard a ringing sound.
All the chatter and words,
I have not heard.
Muffled
By that terminal crunch
Of earth that

Goetz

Clogged my ears,
Because my roots grew
Upside down.
So ig'nant and indignant
I remain,
A shallow mind knows
Nothing but the same.
So seemingly without reason,
My face turns to a frown,
Lamenting the shriveled
Vestige of my roots that grew
Upside down.

Larry Griffin

Heat Wave

Just when all needs to cool, so
I find heat hotter than the past,
and I turn up the cold to know
from what from this now last,
this best artificial wind in my hair--
all blows around in the enclosed air:
I recall Francis, feed my birds and my fish
and birds chirp their wish at that their dish;

and, yet the sun shines down into full force
until a buzzing fly beats my ear; of course,
I take him down into oblivion in the room,
too much evil by his presence, now his tomb.
In this now empty place, my canary sings.
I hear prayer call, as the church bell rings.

White Spirit Bear Vanishing

this bear is not a symbol
neither is its vanishing (*banishing*)
that's the point

vanishing that is
into the edge of the painting
folded down like a sheet
the sides of the canvas
stapled to the wood frame

framed into vanishing (*banishing*)
by greed & profit

a hole punched through the canvas

white spirit bear pushed to the edge
of the canadian island
every fourth black bear
born is white
a genetic miracle
brown-eyed, not albino
not a freak, a gift

clearcutting the northern rainforest
for trees, for paper to print this poem
the bear leaps out at you
its whiteness freezing you
its fleeting omnnipresence
paralyzing you
whitewashing the empty canvas

in my dream it was white
the bear vanishing into the white
staining the world, stunning

Harris

a rainbow of white arching
over this gray vista
hologram just visible
from certain angles
holy light filtered by spectrums
I see stretching forever across this page

white spirit bear concerns me
converging & crashing in the forest
with no one to hear

white spirit bear wants me
I know this as it crosses the tundras
of my peripheral vision

white spirit bear
stalks the corners
of my REM cycles

where the dream is not a symbol
it's a long-distance call

from the rim
of the compass

vanishing (*banishing*)
the bear points home

Poet Nancy Harris

Rodney Jones

DIRTY BLUES

This young living legend leaning
Over the sink of the washroom
Of the Maple Leaf Bar
Was not twenty minutes ago
Blowing the steel bolts out of
The Twelve bars of "Stormy Monday."
Now I imagine he has
Come in from whatever
He kept briefly in the back seat
Of a buddy's parked car
To wash the fresh sediment
Of the flooding of the river Benus
From the skin of his prepuce.
Or is he just now anointing
Himself for some mystical
Communion to commence
Shortly in the scented
Cathedral of a stranger's mouth?
In a minute he will return
For the last set, the songs
So much alike, the women
Dancing with the women,
And the men lighting joints
In the courtyard where
The poet is buried. Just now
The way he goes at it
So carefully, from the tip
Back to the shaft, I think
He might be a stockbroker
Wiping a crust of salt
From the pores of a pair
Of expensive black wingtips
Before going in to purchase
Ten Thousand shares
Of Microsoft. I know

Jones

It is none of my business
Where he comes or goes,
To what perilous conference
In the mean streets
Of the erogenous zones,
But I will tell my friends
Who wait at the oak bar,
Who will still be laughing
When again his music
Begins to darken inwardly.
This song he plays now
Is nothing but the blues.

Artist Sara Beth Wildflower celebrating life
shortly before her death.

Daredevil Poetry

This poem is not like a motorcycle
Poised
To charge up a ramp
And soar
Over an abyss
To land
Just at the lip
On the far side
And spin triumphantly
To a stop

The poem
In fact
Could fail
In whole or part
And still the poet would survive
To try the ramp
Another day

A poem is not a struggle for life
Or death
All hanging
On the proper timing
Of a metaphor

And yet
The thrill is there
And the suspense
The call
To soar over an expanse
Is irresistible

I look straight ahead
I feel the purr of the engine's power

Ivker (Cont'd)

Between my legs
And I go for it
Time and time again

It gets into my blood
It does
To cross gullies and gorges
In a single verse
To head for Arizona
At long last
To take the Grand Canyon
With inches to spare
And ride off
The desert wind
Whipping through my hair
And tomorrow
To return
My hands waving wildly in the air
And reach the other side
Perhaps
Or crash and burn

Julie Kane

Elegy for Poe's Mourner

This year, the black-veiled
Figure who left cognac and
Roses on Poe's grave

Failed to show to mark
His birthday, with the frozen
Earth of Baltimore

Disturbed above your
Own fresh grave; and I clicked from
The news links that claimed

You were Poe's mourner
To tribute sites where friends had
Posted anecdotes

About you: tall, dark,
Heathcliff-handsome charmer of
Grizzled tugboat crews,

Sweet-talking harbored
Ships into stopping work to
Steam-whistle your tunes.

Friends of yours recalled
How you once got pink-slipped for
Making college art

Students paint with their
Own shit; how you rolled onto
Stage in a wheelchair,

Jammed a gun to one
Temple, fired it, slumped, maimed, not
Knowing blanks could kill.

Kane (Cont'd)

When your doctor-dad
Sent you letters calling you
A "n'er-do-well," you

Shot some full of holes,
Set fire to others, then found
A trendy downtown

Gallery to mount
A show, shouting "ATTENTION!"
On your megaphone.

That megaphone was
Why I noticed you at a
Maple Leaf reading;

I was drunk and loved
Crazy men then (still do). But
Our first date began

In near-normalcy:
A Yankees exhibition
Baseball game in the

Superdome, where, when
A foul ball flew into the
Stands, you dove for it:

Kerplunk, heroic!
We carried that ratty ball
All night, through the bars.

Somehow that date stretched
Out for days. You spun your
Rolodex in search

Kane

Of Emmylou's un-
Listed number—who had a
Rolodex at home,

But you? You claimed Jim
Morrison had been your friend,
Then said you were Jim.

I began coming
Down with something: the flu or
Surreality.

When I tried to sleep,
You pried my eyelids open,
Made a puppet speak;

You wound up music
Boxes, shook jingle bells as
They must do in hell.

I got away from
You at last, though you left a
Leather jacket in

My closet with a
License older than you'd said.
You got let go from

UNO, went home
To Baltimore, I guess—and
Then this news you'd passed.

"Rest in peace," say your
Closer friends, but what I wish
For you is that you

Pace in constant
Agitation at the end of
A curly phone cord,

The likes of which will
Also not be seen again.
You were too wild for

Me in that decade
When the bucking bronco rides
In bars would fling us

Mindlessly aside.
Now that I have years to sleep,
I dream you alive.

Maria M. Kelson

Life Is All Present Tense

The piano man's voice is run over gravel because all those rocks at the bottom need their polish and clean—he's so white he's almost albino but the skin he was born in is the only wrong note he hits—this man whose hands run up and down hours of practice and learning, watching, listening and playing to be able to let it all go free.

Here in New Orleans, Pere Antoine came for the inquisition and stayed for the beignets, not exactly, but he returned advocating tolerance and

I have to look up from my notebook every time the drummer hits the crash ride

We're still here, the musicians say, it's our playing, remember, floating all the boats in this city, it's every note, hit, brushstroke, word, dance step anyone ever played has an entire city bobbing on top, and not all the time, but right now is what I mean, not all the time,

I mean now

hopping along, life really is a light frenzy for nothing, the train never stops here, so keep playing

I do not drink

All of the time, not all the time, but I mean now, now

I'm two sazeracs in and

All of a sudden I know what the drunk knows

That a clarinet not only makes love, it makes a river,

and the hands on that piano man are birds that only sing at
night so I can walk on it, the water, and see the full moon booze-
loves me like I booze-love New Orleans, making all kinds of

promises to her, swaying down the street and swearing I want
to meet her parents and hear her secrets cause I know my own
soul was born here, not all the time, but now, I mean now, it is
born here this instant now,

And now don't y'all judge, I know you were all tourists here
once, EVERY one, even those whose first breath still hangs in
this air, has a first-time-drunk-in-the-Quarter story and if it's not
a story, it's a subconscious barge in the river of the mind
curving around the Mississippi's hips

I know you were there, you came with me to Razoo to hear
Phunky Monkey on Bourbon Street, and yes, that's Phunky
spelled with a Ph dropped so low you could grow azaleas from
the concrete

And there's what's his name with his fiddle on the corner, what
is his name, it's just one word, I want to say Shelter, but it's
another word, another leap, another beat, Acadian bourbon
Frenchmen blaze tower bliss tolerance

That's his name, Tolerance James, which is still only one word,
in the all words are one word, sazerac, sense

because if life ain't one long holiday for shaking your head at
the crazy ways of America—one long holiday for listening to the
reanimated vocals of Armstrong on a bench at Fritzels and then
come Sunday watching your soul be born into the battering ram
of the NFL my head to your head your thoughts to my thoughts,

well if that don't just beat, if now is not the gravel getting
polished by time, if you and I are not the scariest funniest

Kelson

hungriest smartest most clueless bunch of skeletons the dead
have ever seen rushing the cemetery gates, then who is, what
is, and I don't mean now, I mean all the time.

(Under the full moon, September 2016, watching Richard Scott and the
Fritzel's New Orleans Jazz Band at Fritzel's European Jazz Pub on Bourbon
Street.)

Les Kerr

Inspiration and Bar Scotch

He could read for umpteen hours, summoning his powers
To conjure up the syllables that kept us all enthralled
Words were his best friends; they were with him at the end
When he said, "He was a mess," was how he'd like to be recalled

On that barstool toward the right at the Maple Leaf each night
He quoted Twain and Shakespeare verbatim, as we watched
New Orleans royalty, the King of Irony
Eighty-proof-strong poetry
Inspiration and Bar Scotch

A distinguished man of letters, I've never seen one better
He could climb out of his mind and into yours on just a phrase
From New Yorker magazine to the streets of New Orleans
He chose drinking and strong thinking as the way to spend his days

It wasn't just the words, but the way he used to say 'em
That brought you in to know the joke on life that he was playin'

By the time I came to know him the seeds that he'd been sowing
Had rooted deep and deadly and spread with kudzu haste
Still, out of the dark shot his bright creative spark
With his pen, he proved his life was no American waste

Lyrics are ©2015 by Les Kerr
Song on **Contributor** cd

Poet Everette Maddox

MADDOX
c/o LEAF
8316 OAK ST
NOLA 70118

LES KERR
111 OLD HICKORY BLVD SW

Singer/songwriter Les Kerr playing
"Inspiration & Bar Scotch" in honor of
poet Everette Maddox.

Blog by Les Kerr

Someone said he had borrowed the suit he was wearing from his brother. The distinguished but declining poet from New Orleans was the special guest at a poetry series in Mobile called Second Saturdays at the Lumber Yard Café. He mesmerized the packed house that day with a book of poems in his hand, a glass of Scotch beside him and a microphone before him. That was Everette Maddox, mid-1980s.

I had first met Everette before then in his natural habitat, the darkened Maple Leaf Bar in New Orleans late one night after JazzFest. He was holding court at the bar with his buddies and admirers, quoting poetry to them over the din of the crowd and music from the next room. Everyone stood as close as they could in order to hear him. "This is a rare man," I remember thinking.

I will always be thankful to my friends Max Reed and Peter McGowin for introducing me to him. I was about to fly the corporate coop into the wide open spaces of music and freelance writing. Everette and others of his independent creative bent were heroes to me then, as they are today. It impressed me that he held songwriters in high regard. Respect from Everette didn't depend on fame or "who you were," it only mattered to him that you were writing. I was writing songs and we became friends

We had a cheerful, fun friendship, not a deep, soul-sharing one. I never felt close enough to him to call him, "Rette," as others did. But when we communicated in person or by postcard, I always felt that each of us shared an admiration for the other as people and as writers. As a performer myself I was immediately impressed with his ability to deliver a poem, an introduction or a passing comment in his uniquely entertaining way. If they were smart, other purveyors of the spoken word took mental notes when they heard him read. Everette wove syllables, sentences and the silence in between them into moments that made listeners forget everything else in the world or even within their own existences when he spoke.

Our conversations included reminiscences of his boyhood in Prattville, Alabama, mine in Mississippi and how much we both enjoyed Nashville. He once started a sentence I was able to finish when we talked about the beautiful view from Interstate 65 North just inside the Tennessee state line when the fields around Pulaski come into view. I always remember that exchange when I'm driving back from the Gulf Coast to Nashville.

Thanks to Peter's suggestion, Everette began inviting me to perform at the long standing Sunday afternoon poetry readings he had founded at the Maple Leaf years before. He would usually have another songwriter or two on those days to add variety to the weekly spoken word event. It was a thrill for me to be a part of those readings and I'm honored that Nancy Harris, who leads the readings now, continues to have me back to sing my original songs on occasion.

Toward the end of his life, he worked feverishly to compile enough poems for another book. Hank Staples, the owner of the Maple Leaf who helped him and held his new poems, mentioned that Everette might like to do a reading in Nashville when it was finished. The notion of Everette staying with me in my apartment would be a possibility if a reading were secured. Everette had heard about the eclectic club on Second Avenue called Windows on the Cumberland, aptly named because of its tall windows overlooking the river. I had played there and said I'd be glad to help, if I could.

But Everette didn't live to see the book published or to make it to Nashville. He died young but full of wisdom in 1989. When *American Waste*, Poems by Everette Maddox was published in 1993, another friend and Everette disciple, Helen Toye, sent a copy to my soon to be wife Gail and me as a wedding present. Her inscription reads, "OK, you two good ones, this one's for you! All the best in your endeavor, Love, Helen."

My favorite poem in the book is called "Mail Box Blues." It's about two mail boxes side by side talking to each other about a postcard made from a torn beer box, destination: New York. The postcards Everette sent to me only went to my one bedroom apartment in Nashville. But when I read them now, in a split second they take me back to a darkened New Orleans bar presided over by a somewhat inebriated poet casting a word-spell as broad as a Gulf Coast mullet net over those of us lucky enough to be caught in it.

Danny Kerwick

from **SIT AS DRIFTWOOD**

feeder creek
                downslope
            twist & turn
ice to sea
                ravines sliced
thru shale
                & granite

        *

in bucket
a nest of words

hook & cast into air
whitecapped & darkdeep

        forget them for now

sit as driftwood
a driftwood conference

no one say anything
silent multitudes

gulls statue on pier

O Canada or O Jamaica
Or small lake
        In the middle of Nebraska

*

raise head
                open eyes
        sun at apex
to fall along horizon

        clear as hum
        clear as church bells
        clear as wind & sand

the air spoke
words big as smoke
as smoke dissipates
one foot in front of the other

        *

one drop of water from faucet
spring rainfall   snowmelt
gushing aquifers on hilltop
By Gold Pennsylvania
NY stateline in sight
msy flow east
Along Susquehanna
To Chesapeake Bay
Or west along Allegehny
Ohio River   Mississippi
To Gulf of Mexico

Kerwick

or north
Thru deep ravine
Dropping 800 feet
Genesee river valley
To Lake Ontario

Where man sits as driftwood
On sandy beach

Bill Lavender

from *surrealism*

15

the city is a church
(here are the people)
we worship at the bar
we witness at the bar

we're pissed off
at each other
for fucking up the church
for fucking up the city

but the city in that sense
is as far from me and you
as dante street from erato
farther

the city we create
in our fury
a place to be exiled
a mirror

22

all that lovely licking
but stamps are
no longer necessary

after a while
the people in the city
the people in the bars
forget that they exist

why there's no longer
a surcharge
even for international

though nations still act
just as heartlessly

and to deliver
becomes a metaphor

delivering a metaphor

24

fire is the business
of fire
love love

what dances above
the unspoken
lump
that is the city

the city has no
business with the city
but with poetry yes
with poems
and with poets

Poet Bill Lavender reads during **The New Orleans Poetry Festival**. Lavender and Megan Burns co-founded the event. The next one is April 20-22, 2017.

Poet Danny Kerwick reads from a new collection, ***Behind Lies the Sugar***.

Black

"I imposed black; it is still going strong today, for black wipes out
everything else around."
Gabrielle Coco Chanel, 1883-1971

1895
Aunt L— cups your small chin, flames a slut-lamp to better see
the future
in your eyes: a convent-orphanage at Aubazine, lessons
orderly as a sampler of stitches, tiny Roman crosses
will a milliner, a seamstress make.
Simple white shirt for your simple chest, schoolboy
necktie, a straw boater plain as a uniform.

1910
You work late, Gabrielle, hemming
 a customer's skirt when the sudden bark of a stray dog startles
the needle from your fingers — you look to the window —
Maman's face in a moon pocked with silver pins. How
long did you sit with Maman's body?

1919
Black wipes out everything else —
The lover you shared with his English wife,
his death mourned by the outlaw of light at the Bel Resprio,
walls painted beige, shutters lacquered shut
waves of black unstopped: the colour of mourning
sewn inside out and lined with cornflowers, poppies, messages
embroidered in daisies. You cut a dress from a pattern
of shadows,

Lawrence

a sheath with trumpet sleeves, raw edges
plain-seamed and pressed to your lips.
Black wipes out everything else —
Does it, Gabrielle? What happens when the black line
dissolves and you're not afraid of the question? How long did
you sit with her body?

Rain bleeds the colour from every hemline in Paris —
those reds, those greens, those electric blues made me feel ill,
wind blowing over, blowing past —
a pendant of scissors dangling from the cord around your neck,
cutting along the edges of everything you long for —

In this room you stretch cloth, baste a waistband,
rip out a collar – stand it higher, stab the air with your cigarette
and orders:
         couture is muscle and skin.

1935
Pencil sketches rescue the evening purse, the clutch that van-
ishes from taxicabs, slips
between couch pillows until you fasten a brilliant gold chain to
the shoulders of fashion.
Gabrielle, who comes to your rescue? Escorts you through the
flaming colours of Paris?
Dances with you at the Waltz Ball? Admires your dropped-waist
black taffeta gown, black pillbox—
Who feeds your wit? Invites you to dine, party? Sends you bou-
quets of white camellia?

Scissors, needle and tailor's chalk.
Undone, re-done, done up, over
and over, a dream pinned to a mannequin.
How long Gabrielle?

Lawrence (Cont'd)

1954
Your new collection,
worn by stem-necked American models, shoulders rolled back,
hips thrust.
They roam the runway in matte jersey suits, mousseline,
    crystal-pleated chiffon gowns,
    gowns of white lace trimmed with red
    red lace edged with metallic thread, seed pearls, jet —

1971
More pins than scissors.
More scissors than thread.
More thread than breath.

    You ride a white horse to Maman
at rest in a one-room cottage in the market town of Brive-a Gail-
larde. Your satchel packed:
dresses, skirts, coats, sewn for women around the world to fall
in love
with themselves —Wallis, Marilyn, Jackie, Liz —

Is it too late to size Maman for a little black dress, a navy-blue
jersey wool suit? Is it too late
to tell her that flesh flows from the bone?
How long, how many years,
did you sit with her in the gathering dusk
alone —

(Italicized lines are from Coco Chanel: The Legend and The Life
by Justine Picardie)

Carolyn Levy

Muscle Pullings

"Muscle pullings Mom. I'm having muscle pullings."
She had just asked, "What's the matter with you?"
Muscle pullings -- that's what they felt like -- my muscles
Pulling inside of me -- not for me but against me.

Of course, I know now, it was serotonin.
My brain had manufactured too much and my body
Was in revolt. But in those days, long ago, they didn't
Talk of serotonin because they didn't know.

Four hundred years since Shakespeare died;
Cervantes a few days later, but back then they had
Muscle pullings. It shows up in black and white.
Mankind has endured them all along, this plight.

I like "tension" now -- it's loaded. Just like muscle pullings are.
Just like too much serotonin. Just like too many night stars.
Just like pay your dues -- you've got to. Just like dream the
Impossible dream. Just like I think I'm going to scream.

'Cause it's tension -- bloody tension. That's the word --
Le bon mot juste. It's tension, bloody tension,
It's how one turns it loose that makes the drama
Of one's earthbound sojourn, long or short.

It's tension -- bloody tension -- freedom from it divine.
To put to use its demons, to drink a goblet of wine.
To make love in the daylight, to make love in the night.
It's tension -- bloody tension -- that's what it is alright.

Top: Poet Megan Burns reads during New Orleans Poetry Fest.
Bottom: Poet BJ Ward from New Jersey.

Top: Caroline Levy, author of *Regina;* Bottom: Marjorie Maddox, author of *Weeknights at the Cathedral*.

The Poem

It's a rug: jump
on a bump and
another humps

up. It won't stay
smooth. It's nice skin
that keeps breaking

out in boils. It's
a cathedral,
with every word

a little gar-
goyle. A big grin
with all the teeth

snaggled. Because
somewhere, down deep
inside, every-

thing is not all
right.

Margaret Marley

To Aunt Jeanne, With Love

You and Jean always welcomed us kids to tea.
We knew you were a couple very early
But it never mattered, never seemed weird,
Around you two my mom was also quite well reared.
Jeanne, you gave me my first Nancy Drew!
My second crime novel is so in memory of you.

When Jean passed away you fell quite sad
I don't blame you with the adventures --
as far as Egypt you and Jean had
Jeanne, you and Jean had one of the healthiest
relationships I've known.

Jeanne's whole life she believed in ghosts
So I hope now she and Jean happily haunt
their shared home.

Francinister

We've always had each other if not anyone else.
We share each other's secrets and sorrows
          and have each other's backs.
We've spent hours and years playing pranks
          on Dad for the amusement of ourselves.
If anyone ever fucks with you
I'll bludgeon his dumb ass.

Sometimes we chow down on pizza:
I have my vodka, you your beer --
Watching our current Netflix obsession
          all evening in a proper smoky room.

We laugh like hell at Dad's goofiness
and confide in each other without fear.
Enjoy your cans of La Croix
          before passing out at my bed's foot --
A curled up fair-faced gargoyle
          warding off all doom.

My little Sis, Francinister,
Life long partner in crime,
Most darling of the dears!

Maggie Marley sings inside the Maple Leaf on a rainy Sunday. Bottom: Haiku Society performers Karel Sloane-Boekbinder, Juliet Seer Pazera, and Robert Allen.

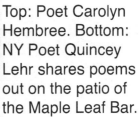

Top: Poet Carolyn Hembree. Bottom: NY Poet Quincey Lehr shares poems out on the patio of the Maple Leaf Bar.

Top: Writer Mark Marley reads a short-short story. Bottom: New Orleans novelist Vicki Salloum reads from *Faulkner & Friends*.

Lesson

As a kid I got a BB gun.
Shot out the street light
With shot number one.
Then aimed at everything
That made its way on wings.
Until one gray day
I stalked a sparrow on a wire.
Perhaps because its eyes were set wide
Or because its was unwise
Regarding beastly boys
It seems I was not seen
And shot it in the fluggy chest
Where there appeared
A drop of blood quite red
As it hung there by tiny talons dead
That I might never kill again.

Pensacola

The beach is fine
If you don't mind
A huge metaphor
For the unconscious mind
And the ceaseless creation
And dissolution of the universe
Breathing down your neck
Around the clock.

Michael Martin

Secrets

Like batteries and most of your sea fish,
They're disappointed when they're dead.
Like us, they probably thought
Death to be, something, you know, 'not-life.'

It's what we hear when we sleep, secrets
Pounding out in dead language
How they keep on keeping on,
How this is for your ear only;
What happens in Vegas, stays in Vegas....

But this morning—in the only home
We've known, high on its stilts
Overlooking the only beach we've ever
Taken the time to fall for—

We rise again and count the children.
We grind the beans and feed the guppy.
Like an Energizer Bunny,
Banging our little drum.

Car Wreck Outside The Dinner Party

In the end, it took only a horn blast to turn
the acreage over. Despair, the New Machinery—
all that stuff would no longer catch the ear.
We bad-vibed the plows into congregating
somewhere outside our view of the collision.
The dinner rolls left before the butter arrived
and then that general feeling of
free-floating general something
stepped inside.
We stared at the children.
What made us name them all Dylan?
Why so easily aggrieved, the wives of the Great Authors?
"He's written more books than he's read you know
and he's only written two."
We went back to chewing the meat.
Can Juan get my hair to do that?
Did I just live the life of someone I don't know?
Look at us. Carefully setting the correct fork
next to the end of the world.

Top: Karel Sloane shares a heartfelt poem on the dance floor of the Maple Leaf. Bottom: Poet/editor Michael Martin from North Carolina speaks during a presentation for his collection of poems titled ***Extended Remark***.

Top: Writer Nina Ouedraogo & friend perform a duet reading.
Bottom: Poet Laura Mattingly.

Charlotte Mears

Malaise and Beyond

When everything finally has stilled and become mute
the moon hangs in windows as a heart skips a beat,
slips into jazz scat panicked, half-woken and unknowing
where? which city? which bed? A reel of images projects
onto the inside lid of an eye in search of answers, of mapping—

A large windowed loft, the bed shared with a lover in an
        uncluttered space.
The gas heater and damp cinder-block walls of a cramped
        one-bedroom apartment.
Or a childhood bedroom wallpapered in repeated, dream-like
        gardens still-floating.
Rooms in cities long forgotten except for the smell of urine
        or gardenia in bloom.
Where is "Here" at any given moment? But sometimes—

Just sometimes when histories finally merge at once
the heart's storage opens as a face turns in greeting,
raises the moon's morning, its conquerable waking
into full-throated lyric and song so rare, so beautiful,
so worth it all for that shining second beyond confusion—

Robert Menuet

The Piper Keens Out Grace

The Chiaroscurist's mist dissolves the arc of the horizon,
steel grey of water, blue steel of morning sky;
young pelicans fish low in waters warmed near flood pumps.
Pull away from the rushes now, for in a ray of light
the particles of dust stream down
upon Lake Pontchartrain that promise good,

but poised in deadly still the hour
the sun forebears to shine
a coil-sprung tail of red decay washes
from the spillway with hyacinth leaves.
A wretched crow shuttles cross
the levee above an armadillo's rigor-curl;
it dips a heel of French bread in the brine,
it flies past reeds and snares to rest and feed.

One windless day soon after your estrangement
the brown goose closed her unfurled wings,
lost her liftoff from the listing pile;
as from the second row you did the weeping,
they laid your brother-husband out, your shield and portion,
beneath the grape vine in the garden room,
his liver exploded like pinecone clatter on paving stone.

The crow alights upon the highest branch
and sits and calls to batture rooks;
they gather as a bark of alligator hide
drifts near the irises and cypress knees.

Top: Trey Shreves recites a poem from memory. Bottom: Cheryse Williams reads a poem.

Two poets sharing their poetic art during an open-mic session.

89

Michael "Quess?" Moore

Grounded by Sky: A Southern Epitaph

knowing that I walk atop the bones of my ancestors
in the shadow of their oppressors
towering statuesque above me

I cannot look down without feeling
the puzzled pieces of my past
beckoning me back together
cannot look up without feeling
the weight of history break me into pieces

I cannot leave this ground & feel whole
cannot stand it either
without its heavy sky
pummeling my dreams into nightmares

the ground is a haunt
is a restless cauldron of simmering spirits
bubbling over beneath the soles
of callous sojourners singed
by the heat beneath their feet
yet numb to the stories in its foment

the sky is riddled in dead eyes
the probing gaze of ghastly me
now ghosts cast into iron

who when flesh
owned men, women & children my kin
who when flesh
beat men, women & children my kin
who when flesh
raped men, women & children my kin
who when flesh
slaughtered, maimed, murdered

"Quess?"

men, women & children that looked like me

I cannot leave this ground
where the scattered bones of my ancestry
lay namelessly
without tomb nor headstone
sans burial ground much less monument
& not feel the echoes of a chorus
of gnashing teeth testimonies
hissing at my heels

can not stand this ground
without feeling
the frozen laughter of gilded antebellum
the sky a glacier of silence
that yet speaks so loudly

if you dare to listen closely
you'll hear their names
whispering proclamations of self praise
from the perch of street signs
that hang like still nooses
suspended in time
lynching the esteem of listless passersby
the stories beneath their feet
& above their heads
having passed them by

yet the themes having ground their weight
into their subconscious
making of their minds infertile soil
insufficient to nourish the seeds of dreams
for the dead eyes have probed
& made lifeless the soil
the bones have spoken
but their voices have been muted
by the cast iron gaze above

I live in New Orleans
where the bones of my ancestors
beat the ground like a drum
bang Bamboula rhythms
through the soles that walk this land

I live in the South
where monuments to Robert E. Lee
PGT Beauregard & Jefferson Davis
stand taller than most homes
& the street signs
are noosed in the names of slavers

I cannot leave this ground & feel whole
cannot stand it either
& not feel history
trying to break me
on its cyclic wheel

Geoff Munsterman

Revival

He wasn't used to stars. He dreamed they fell.
He dreamed they swarm him in a
warm summer should've been the fall
by now & guzzle blood that's half his mama
cooking necks on hot plates propped
next to her velvet bed decorated with
bones from lovers lace their boots too tight
& half his father whoever he was.

His welts massive as the jazz catalog
the library still wants six bucks for
but he could give six hecks since
it made him happy mastering St. Louis
Blues on the old piano in his head.

He dreams he's dead. Heart scarred
like the rivertowns south of Orleans
leaning into Mississippi like
vines blackberry dense.

He dreams the oil came alive one June
& wore a funny porkpie hat
brim bursting with purple feathers.
Says his name is Jim, but everyone
leaves his tent swearing his name
is Zombstradamus since he made
that cripple Charleston & that blind
man's eyes like telescopes & brought
 the dead back to life like it was
simple as breath to undo death.
Stars suck him drier than
an arsonist's conscience,
their knotty wings & proboscises
throbbing luminescent,
burning white like firefly asses

& since he's just husk he's hushed
till Jim arrives & taps his blistered
shoulders telling him to come inside
the tent a bit & get himself revived.

The low moon grown lonely blinks
& resurrects the starry night—blazes
a sky usually purpled by plants spew
their charred clouds all over us, spew
what cooked the sky of stars in the first place.

His home becomes the worst place:
the hit-first place, the disgrace place,
the run out fast as you can place
& yet that first night ever seeing stars
teaches him his place—
he hadn't left it yet & knew
it was too late to ever leave it now.

And his father was the river running off.
And his mama always told him
dreaming of a better life than
what you're given is a sin, that
the world will always win
& if you look up expecting to jump up
you'll get smacked down.

So he grows up & don't once think
better comes & doesn't once wish
for anything which is why he
wasn't used to looking up at stars.

The pollutant isn't only in the sky,
the water, the dirt beneath you if you let it in you—
there will always be a reason not to
look up at the stars, always a voice

Munsterman

demanding that you kneel & bow
& crack your spirit like a grimace
driven to concrete.

No one ever told him that if a bug
bites & you still feel it, you're alive.
That you don't ever let them let you think you're dead.
Which is why full-bellied stars rise up
& brine the sky with the salt
of all he had within. Which is why
all his life he just wasn't ever used to stars.

Geoff Munsterman

Nine Blueprints From the Son of a Carpenter

The house you were raised in
was built on weekends
by the friends and family received
his carpentry for free. Every day
for seven months, he would leave a job
site to work in lamplight, hard at
what the others couldn't do.
Each lumberyard board
handpicked—details designed
like an obsessive god
and carried out by
the same blood pumps
your veins. It is never your
house as much as it is his.

Find yourself eyeing roadside piles
and construction dumpsters for
the jigsaw scraps you could fit
together into a life. You will see them,
you will know what they are,
and then you will remember you
thought you were too good to
learn how to use them.

Calloused hands held you
the day you were born.

You will know what sunlight does
to bright bodies—how his crisp bacon skin
is nothing resembling even
your darkest freckle. You will know sweat
maims a cotton shirt, leaves
nothing but a warped collar;
that a shirt drying on the picket

takes its shape, is pulled off
harder than a scab.

Engineers don't know shit. Got degrees
out the ying yang and still
designs a bathroom with
four walls and no damn entrance
then yells at the men for
straying from the plans.

Childhood smells like sawdust, sounds
like a steady hammer driving
nails through 2x4s. Your jeans sag,
heavy with a phantom
tool belt awkward on your hip.

You know what he looks like
in tighty whiteys. He eats dinner
in his tighty whiteys, watches Star Trek in
his tighty whiteys—even if your prissy aunt
expects him to go put clothes on, even if
your brother's new girlfriend comes by
unannounced, he will answer the door wide
in his tighty whiteys, say Come on in.
His near nudity is the only thing to
break the fever of his workday.

You will never hire a carpenter
decent enough—the cut
corners of lesser men termite
your bank account. You will not
be able to sit through
remodeling shows without a ghost
in tighty whiteys yelling for Bob Vila
to do it cheaper or better.

Overpriced bids and home
improvement shows, how-to
handbooks and handy tips
stepfather your memories.

You walk into a room, remember
how he could measure it
within a sixteenth of an inch
with his eyes. The numbers
will not come to you, the room
will contract and expand,
immeasurable.

Biljana D. Obradović

A Hierarchy of Names

My nephew says in Italy, where he lives, they call
non EU people extracomunitario, a pejorative word.
In Greece, he introduces himself to Italian tourists, his clients,
as Sean O'Brady, not Dušan Obradović, which is his real name,

and they in turn think of him as an Irishman—a good thing, not a Serb.
When the once US Poet Laureate, Charles Simic came to the US, he
changed his name from Dušan to Charles and removed the funny
       mark on the c.

When a family with my last name came through Ellis Island
on their way to Omaha, Nebraska, at the turn of
the twentieth century they changed their name to O'Bradovich,
making it more Irish, which must have been
       what the officers presumed it was
because of the masses of starving Irish people emigrating to America.

I didn't want to change my name when I became a citizen.
But I often wonder if I should have taken my husband's name
and become Billie Ann O'Gery (or taken his old name Dougherty),
become Billie Ann O'Dougherty, very Irish, very American.

But, I'd need to keep the O as a memory of what used to be there,
what used to be my name before I was urged to assimilate
or be constantly looked down upon as a foreigner.
In a drawer in my office I keep cutouts from envelopes or letters

addressed to me with my misspelled name. It happens all the time.
I am quite surprised at all the possibilities for misspellings,
and now even get excited at the prospect of yet another one, like:
Obradovie, O'Bradovic, or Biljara, Bilhana, Bilzanan or Bityana

But, I did not add my husband's name to mine, nor did I add
an h to the end of my last name to make it more American.
       Obradović

Obradović (Cont'd)

Let people struggle, keep asking how to spell it,
    how to pronounce it.
Perhaps my name will become memorable and one day
    they will all know how to spell my name and I won't have
to do anything anymore about it.
Perhaps they will want to name their children after me one day, or not.
Transform, blend in—is the last thing I want to do.
I don't mind being different, standing out, being weird,
just being myself.

Nina Ouedraogo

Congo Square, New Orleans, 1843

In Prudence's eyes flames flutter,
Flicker red and yellow flattering one the other.
The drummers' hands beat to the fire in her feet
All those individual pyres over centuries.
Woe to the unknowing of the revenge
Change exacts. Prudence dances reversal,
A message from Erzulie Gé Rouge.
The change who knows its name claims space
According to the lessons of time.
Prudence collapses.
The drums dare remember a place
They name only to themselves,
Ask mercy.
Constance steps slow into the circle,
Her hips a scale rocking two weights at war.
Constance dances in a gown of little white flags,
Foam of waves, she is a daughter of Yemaya,
Queen of the empire the infinite ocean is.
She waves scarves cool blue, down and up
As if sprinkling water.
The change which needs time
Is the change which wants peace.
The drummers' hands mirror the sea
When the sun shines on it silver, easy with heat.
Constance twirls the ocean's ripples in the wake of bodies
Dropped to lighten a greedy load.
Prudence on the ground opens her eyes.
It is then Benedicte dances into the circle,
Daughter of Oshun of rivers, she has peacock feathers,
As if an offering to all who can see. The rocking of her hips
Is the pleasure of sugar water in lemon juice.
Benedicte shares her feathers with Constance;
Benedicte, a sister come to help in a time of difficulty.
Constance and Benedicte caress Prudence with the feathers.
The drummers' hands are the Mississipi, brown waves and ducks
Asking the sky which way to go with each movement of wind.

Kay Murphy

Family Talent Shows

My sisters and I left our father's house
with, yes, terror; it took us ten years.
Four of us married, as was required;
three of us divorced in the same year;
two remarried, divorced, remarried again.
One had a papal annulment after
four children. Between us, we have
twelve children; I still count
the one dead. Five are females.
Among us is one born again, one
Catholic, one atheist, one Buddhist.
Two went to college, one worked
in a factory until it closed. One sold
drugs until she was caught; now
she sells See's candy in California.
Two of us suffer migraines, two reflux,
two arthritis; our doctors say we are
long livers. Two of us have been in jail,
one in detox, and one in a state
hospital for the incurably insane.
One of us has a tic that makes her
count things to make sure they're still here.
If you come to the family reunion
you won't know one of us from the other.
If you stay for the talent show, I do
Elvis impersonations, and my born-
again sister impersonates me. The two
performances look eerily alike.
Three of us will harmonize "Sugar
In the Morning," although our father
demanded we sing it when he was drunk.
My brother-in-law will perform funerals
in which the deceased, like it or not,
take Jesus into their heart.

Murphy

Me, I'm going to be cremated.
My mother will read a rhymed
and metered poem she composed.
It's always funny, but we always cry.
If you look for me, I'm the one
who looks absent, like our father.
But that won't help you because
he is dead, which is why we can
now come back to our mother's home.

Melinda Palacio

Bones for Feathers

Was it the whistlers egging you on, daring
you to take one final plunge,
their trilling whistle like zeal and applause
and love you've always longed for?
Oh, those sienna ducks,
northern migrants to New Orleans like you.
Not a goose of the safe, everyday kind,
but a flighty, spontaneous bird.
Snappy, someone called you.
Was it a compliment? Who cares.

Days turned to night-filled adventure
down Bourbon street and upriver.
That warm spring and sultry summer
a hazy blur until perfect fall weather.
How friendly everyone was at first.
Food and drink aplenty.
When your money ran out,
the faces staring back at you changed.
Some wanted to lock you up,
medicated in a padded cell.

No room for loonies or loners,
lucky for you, said the shelter.
A lanky lady with less than trustworthy,
marbled eyes warned you to stay safe,
away from shifty campers under the bridge.

Palacio

One day you found yourself
mesmerized by the joggers in Audubon Park.
Where are they all going to as they circle
the green lagoon and loop back again and again?
Blindly following white arrows on concrete,
blanketed in dumb determination.
Groups of women like the flock
of white geese chattering in the corner,
moving as one around the water's edge.

Or perhaps you were wooed by the cob swan
who preens, fluffs his feathers and teases,
as if waiting all this time for you to say,
            this is where I'll end my days.
            In this bird-filled lagoon, I will be your mate.

Your final metamorphoses complete
as you took a victory lap in the lagoon,
then filled your lungs with water,
exchanged your bones for feathers.

Note: On October 10, 2016, NOPD retrieved a body floating in Audubon Park Lagoon.
The deceased was a middle-aged homeless woman who had traveled from Massa-
chusetts. A group of joggers found the drowned woman. There was no evidence of
foul play.

Spike Perkins

A Long Goodbye

sunlight and shadows
filtered by louvered shutters
and ceiling fans, she's sleeping
naked on the bed, a glint
of an empty glass

I'm alone in stirring and working, as
the sun beats and the cicada song
rises and falls, and cloud shadows shift

drinking in the images and sounds
and thoughts, rationalizing the romance
of self-destruction with Faulkner and Baudelaire

is a bourbon-laced Southern dance with death
so different from heroin in Harlem, or opium
in Hong Kong, or absinthe in Paris?

living fast and dying young isn't the only way
to leave a pretty corpse, you can do a slow rhumba
with rum and slip away in late middle age,
and still turn heads the memories of those
who loved you

Top: Jonathan Warren adds a somewhat sacred sound to the poetry reading with his Native American flute. Bottom: Ingrid Pavia reads from her smartphone.

Reincarnation

this life?
this life is a reincarnation
in my other life
i was diabolical
satan's handiwoman
perhaps i was satan
because this life
this life is always on the verge
but it never succeeds
and it is not me
and my foolish humanness
that cause these failures
it is epic storms
 government shutdowns
 shuttered nonprofits
unnatural disasters
insatiable sinkholes
well-placed levee breaks
money-trumped friendships
money due and owed that never showed
 that undying belief in humanity
—utter foolishness really—
that always have me in their clutches

granted, the booming voice
in my head is not always
that kind to me but sometimes
the words are kind,
sweet, strong, beautiful
i begin to feel the possibility
but reality
is the probability
that this voice
and this life mean me

Valentine

no good
no good at all
it has taken me a long time
truly a long time
to see through my hopeful naïveté
to see the true light of this life
is the darkness that surrounds it
i have finally decided
not to keep fighting
to just go with the flow
of always being in this struggle
because i am too much a coward
to take the easy way out

maybe next time, next lifetime
after i have caught up on my dues
i will come back as someone
who makes a difference
at least in my own life

Emma D. Pierson

Mississippi: Where It All Begins

Here is a river
Indian called
running free, untrammeled
from its Minnesota source.

A fluid skein of life
liquidly etching
a continental center
definitely, definitively.

Here, straddled by bridges,
there flanked by wharves
and walls of towns;
now banked by greenness undisturbed:
orchards, forestlands, gardens,
plains, farms, lawns.
Flooding.
Sweeping topsoil
tap roots, trees,
 all before it as an avant garde:
pollutants, toxins,
wastes unspeakable;
noxious outpourings
produced and tolerated
by narrow-visioned venal men.

Engorging
being engorged
by myriad effluvients
pulling all with mute acceptance
into its core.

Symmetrical
always moving, moving always on

Consistent
as in ages unrecounted
it absorbs
the drainage of the land
and flows unhurriedly
toward its goal.

Passing through
southern estuaries
swampy inlets
shaded bayous
shallow marshes
muddy deltas,
making its way
determinedly,
this vivific
wide, brown,
beauteous water
quickens rapidly
in anticipation.

Then, spreading through
its generous mouth,
where, laying its silted burden down,
swirls alluvial riches
in heady release.

Now, the river stills
in warm repose
quiescent to the sun;
and bending and blending
beneath itself,
flings its liquid essence
skyward, high above
the azure reaches of the Gulf.
Mississippi:
where it all begins.

Paul Pines

THE DEATH OF EDDIE JEFFERSON

--for Lisa B.

I was at Eddie's funeral
in Pittsburgh
when they put him in the earth
on a hillside

        overlooking
        a confluence of rivers

Leon Thomas
delivered the eulogy
then sang one of Eddie's favorite
compositions

        Ellington's "Come Sunday"

I stood between Lisa and
"Alto Madness" Richie Cole,
Facing Eddie's wife "Little Bit"
and old friend Irv

all of us in shock

Eddie
who channeled the soul
of Hawkins
Moody
Bird

        tapping out their solos
        with his feet

taken from us
by a crazed gunman

        (the Angel of Death
        a disgruntled hoofer
        with a hit list)

Pines

died
in Richie's lap
on a sidewalk in Detroit
after their gig
at Baker's Keyboard Lounge

Eddie
whose lyrics bridged
continents

           notes
           and syllables

politics
and race

       defined
       what that other Jefferson
       called a "natural
       aristocrat"

at home
before royalty
and in smoke filled rooms
like the Tin Palace
where bebop
met "the Freedom Guys"

       (who shed
       form
       to reform
       from dis/
       sonance)

about which Eddie
said:

       "It evolves, man.
       If you don't sit and listen
       what's the use of being around?"

then cited a passage
in the Upanishads
where creation proceeds
from the Creator's loneliness

this sudden self awareness
              expressed
              in racing syllables
              create
              the world
a sacred vocalese
familiar to the man
who soared on
such solos
              taken from us
              in May 1979
              at 60
I can still see the confluence of rivers
from that hillside

and realize
Eddie discovered in jazz
what Bohr, Heisenberg and Pauli
did in Copenhagen
1935

recording
in the breakdown
of radiated atoms
a new understanding
of the relationship
between matter
and energy
              the unpredictable
              dance
                    of particle
                    and wave...

*Eddie Jefferson, the iconic jazz singer/lyricist, began as a hoofer. He invented vocalese by setting words to bebop solos he first tapped out to preserve. Eddie was shot in Detroit, outside Baker's Keyboard Lounge, on May 8, 1979. He died on the lap of alto player Richie Cole.

Manfred Pollard

Resurrection Visitation:
Ars Poetica: Epiphany Crown

He left me waking to his death as prized
a call then came from my lost brother Dan
who said his father, my step-dad had died
then Dan disclosed his executor plan.
I mentioned that I had had a strange dream
around then, three months back, of soldier dad,
as in his resurrected body's gleam
of vigor in dad's infinite youth, undead.
Surpassing William Blake's sublime, his youth,
a love supreme, no fearsome sense of wrath
to greet me from old noble brownstone's truth
like bright Jerusalem light's amber bath.
I let Dan know of dreadful dreams before
dad's death, cremation with his army honor.
No longer need I see through a family chore
in crisp dark green fatigues from some back door.

In crisp dark green fatigues from some back door,
an army wooden white board hospital wing,
he walked across a ramp transitioning
with several steps to a brownstone porch floor.
As he turned facing me straight down the stairs,
his lingered smile, perfect recognition face
had let me feel the washed out hate displace
his sins in life, purged from him with my fears,
beside his serious gaze in awe at sky.
This breathless place for his transition through
new life, allowed to lead me as I'd try
to gaze on states that happen, what leads to
the next phase living brings after we die,
the grace my eyes were meant to see anew.

The grace my eyes were meant to see anew,
he shared and turned, I followed by his side,
unsaid words felt, from sidewalks we arrived.
A building like the other I looked into,
a few young men touched up near plaster walls,
one kind resembled me in youth, through I moved
in part then walked out, though filled with gratitude,
I was not ready for beyond the halls
or rooms they led to, what they lit to see.
Outside, the city dressed young men and women
who walked about the streets relaxed by me.
Then I drew up to dad as if unseen,
we stood at the next stone porch silently,
he stepped grand steps and through the door was gone.
Internal radiance like fire baptized,
he left me waking to his death as prized.

James M. Robinson

FIRST CLASS WITH EVERETTE MADDOX

It must have been
in one of the older buildings
that replaced the ones
burned down during the Civil War
beneath the Druid oaks
in the central quad.
Since it was January
the vested wool suit
did not seem out of place
nor the old-timey beard,
but the chrome-colored
aluminum rack adhesive-taped
to his forehead, upper cheeks
and nose with a rubber tube
looped into one nostril
beneath the votive candles
of his blackened eyes
could not have been
more strange than his lack
of any explanation
until after an hour and minutes
before we were dispersed
he finally addressed the issue
that had held us in suspense
by waving an open hand
before his afflicted face.
"Oh, this? Don't mind this.
This is just what happens
when you mix a little darkness
with a lot of Scotch."

Top: NY-based poet Paul Pines; Bottom: California-based poet Chryss Yost

Top: Poet James Miller Robinson of Huntsville, Alabama, reads a poem about his former teacher Everette Maddox.
Bottom: Poet Bernard Pearce reads a poem about life along Bayou Teche.

David Rowe

THE DAY ETTA DIED

It's late January, Congo Square, & about
80 muggy degrees out
& just as global warming
Explains this long Indian Summer,
For your gorgeous voice
We've got an ecology of heartache to thank.
On identity's fluidity
Alcoholics & drug addicts all
Agree, & in my stupor
Of grief, I recall
My homeboy Frank
O'Hara's obit billet-doux
To Billie Holiday
& how, if psyche means butterfly
& this dispossessed monarch's
Indeed your soul, then this egret
Can only be Johnny Otis,
The great bandleader who brought
You, a teen runaway, to the world's notice
& then, eager to play
Psychopomp & lead you through the Pearly Gates,
Predeceased you by a day or two.
It was at Jazz Fest here in town
That I first saw you, dear Etta, throw down
& when I say that I cried
I mean something like the time I got maced
By a fed
-up soulmate
With the same damn can of mace I'd
Bought her myself,
                    what I mean
Etta dear, is that I shed
Non-stop & ugly-face tears.

David Rowe

SHADOW, POSSESSION BY MY

Laugh all you like—I practically can myself—but, some months ago now, my shadow jumped into me. Even to call it my shadow, though, traffics in half-truths, to wit: not only did it act autonomously, quite in fact as if I belonged to it, but also the spectral damn entity didn't much resemble me. What's more, it was a poor fit, my stature too small to readily accommodate it, which meant my torment became compounded & protracted as the invasive silhouette thrashed around struggling to settle into my frame, affording me ample time to surmise what exactly in me was being so radically displaced, so profoundly compromised. Perhaps, too, though paralyzed, unable even to scream, my own role wasn't entirely passive or without blame. Had, for example, my inveterate negativity & sorrow actually manufactured the unholy space, the Black Tabernacle for the perverse shadow to occupy? Or, conversely, had my six-plus years of sobriety & relative virtue encouraged an archetypal apparition to embrace me, however brutally, with Delphic Grace? I'll note that while it's true I was lying in bed throughout this admittedly hypnopompic event, to go so far as to dismiss it as a dream would be remiss if only because it's easily the most compelling of my more recent memories. In any case, whether some kind of mystic consummation or nonconsensual astral incest, whether an anthropomorphic anxiety attack or hex crafted by a vexed & vindictive ex, it left me ravaged. I suppose the best spin to give the whole uncanny episode is just to recall that, after all, my people are those who inhabit the thresholds, the thin places, the twilit crossroads...in short, those very souls intimate with shadows.

for Missy

Edgar Sierra

Pipe Dreams

The old man recounted tales
of rivers meandering through jungles
where trees obscure light
from distant Perseus,
quick sands of lizard brain
in the shooting stars of night,

the miasma of rotten woods and swamp
percolating at three a.m.,
when tired limbs surrender,
and carrion flowers feast on flies
beneath the Little Dipper,
and reddish coral reefs protruding like castles
eject the psychedelic dreams
drifting in the sea bed.

Across the icy tundra the love like grass
that never grows in permafrost
reflects a time of life:

Wolverine eyes beyond the timberline,
where drunken souls from northern latitudes
smell like kerosene and whiskey.

Necropolis of kings along the Nile,
the bluish blobs of ink
of letters never send . . .
"forget old grudges," the old man said
smoking his pipe,
"have no regrets . . ."

On Mount Everest
clouds surround the summit . . .

Oxygen

the source of life
in every breath
like time the knife
inviting death

the priestly flame
consumes the rich
oxygen air
when we grow old

spoiling wine
inviting mold
in grape or vine
if you're not there

to share the love.

Poet/storyteller Jimmy Ross

C.M. Soto

PUZZLE PIECING

Every evening, you carry your roped cloth bag to me.
The blue wood pieces pop around inside.
"Let's do puzzles," you say.
I put down the homework—not away, but beside—
and I lend my hands to this ritual.
I watch your grapefruit cheeks as you concentrate.

We share a glass of water.
You say, "excuse me," when you burp,
and I am reminded of the man
who would have made you and I a family.
And we vertically stack these wood parts
together to make some sense of the blue design.
It is a circus seal and you ask me to clap.

I tell you of the time you drank milk from my breasts.
You laugh, talking about bowling with boobs.
You don't yet understand
what it is like to share your body,
but you like bowling—your grandpa Ed bowls.

Finished, you sweep away the pieces
and I fall back into my papers. You watch T.V.
Somewhere between, I've figured our life
is a putting together what must fit,
make sense of it between us,
learn one another all over again.
To guarantee us a few seconds,

every day we assemble the pieces.

Top: Poet Charles "Sulla" Morgan.
Bottom: Linda Leung reads a favorite
poem.

Paris Hughes Tate

November 2 (All Souls Day)

The latest marble tombstone was erected
after he was planted under soil that still fumbles
to reconnect. As always, after the funeral,
he became an abandoned
church—
collected more dust than pews,
and visitors that never noticed a slow
decay
until bones just fatally reduced to crumbling
rubble.
He reunited with his (grudgingly married)
parents and the twin who could have been
a pharmacist until 1996 stopped him. Near
the end, he sided with their last name,
joined their disdain for my red glass
rosary as I beseeched St. Joseph in whispered
corners. Today,
November brushes the withered goldenrods;
they shiver on his above ground grave before
replaced. Black dusted fingers clasp below
the murmured Novena. So in the end, I
latch the rusted metal gate of the cemetery behind
me, and figure this is how we'll reconcile his
deathbed manners.

Top: J.E. Warren plays one of his songs. Below: Poet
Grace Bauer, from the University of Nebraska, reads
during the 1st annual New Orleans Poetry Festival.

Top: Poet Paris Hughes Tate shares a poem.
Below: Melinda Palacio & Steve Beisner after a read-
ing. (In the cozy booth up front at the Maple Leaf).

Lucy Wells Tierney

Under-Minding the Termites

Slowly, below consciousness, termites were dining,
and I was losing my mind.
A thousand hatched, swarmed
from lush habitat,
a cancer upon the house.
Chomping rain-soaked wood,
they've guts to digest a house.

They bear food for the queen.
I do not pledge allegiance to her.

Stealthy as death they
built a horrid nest
of dirt and rotten wood,
glued with spit and shit.

Termites destroy slowly, hidden in the dark, silent,
out of sight, like the mind ages.
I lose one memory at a time, out of mind.
The mind conjures up ideas, disappears thoughts
Then reality intrudes upon the dream.

Nervously, I realize the damage.
I was paralyzed as one disturbing sight
was succeeded by a deeper view of damage,
escaped from fantasy into reality.

To hell with co-existing with nature,
Ahimsa, compassion,
that a death act could boomerang,
that termites decompose dead trees to nourish the living trees.

They eat at my mind, and I rage against the dark,
thousands of termites.

Lucy

I declare trench war: poison foam,
enlisted roofers, my savings, contractors.
I think of Salvador Dali's horror:
bugs crawling over a clock,
so that time melts away beside a corpse.

Bugs walk across a white damask tablecloth
toward some moldy wood,
ignoring the sign IPlease Do Not TouchI.
More march toward a reclining woman.
Bugs file alongside a string of beads
upon a manikin's forehead
as if to steal her mind.

Waitin' for the Light to Change

Well, I was standing at the corner
Of Liberty and State
And it was wait, wait, wait —
The traffic light was stuck on yellow
And like everybody else I was late, late, late —
Waitin' for yellow to turn green

People in autos were stopping and going
Pumping their brakes
North South East and West
Hoping no one coming out of a blind spot
But no one stopped to fix the light
Their signal saying hurry, saying hesitator waits

Lookin' round with an uneasy eye
I glance at a front page pic
Through a plastic windowed metal newsbox
And beneath the static light I see children
Lying face down in a street in the holiest of lands
Through the yellow plastic it's hard to tell
Who launched the rocket
I just pray it wasn't made by In God We Trust

And I'm growin' tired of this waitin'
So I decide to risk it all and make a mad dash
Across the intersection, but soon as I start
I'm bombed with honk, honk, honkin' horns
And somebody hollerin' "Hey, get back up on that curb, boy!"

Well, I'm thinking about this and thinking about that
Thinking of those headlines and those kids
And it occurs to me to climb that metal pole
And bang on that traffic light box up there.
Hey, nobody seems to be awatchin'—

Travis

So, before I know it I'm shimmyin' on up.
Yet soon as I'm up there seems like everybody's watchin'.
Anyway, I bang on it once and then bump it again
But it doesn't respond and I suddenly realize
Its signal's comin' from way over yonder—

Then, just then, I hear wheels screechin' to a halt
And I catch a flash of blue—
Just as I'm slidin' down, you understand—
And the cop says "What you doin' up there, man?"

And I say "Just tryin' to fix the light,
It's stuck on yellow, sir."
"Well, yeah," the cop says, "but you not authorized.
You got to be authorized. I'm sorry but you under arrest.
Tamperin' with the timin' that's serious stuff."

So he hauled me down to jail
And threw me in a cell with three other dudes
One who had a fist in the second guy's face
While the third was off in a corner playin' with himself.
It was hell, man, and I ain't just talking about the smell.

Anyway I'm out of jail now, thanks to bail,
And my lawyer's telling me to just tell it true—
How I was late like everybody else
And just trying to fix the light
Like any good citizen would do.

So wish me luck, if you would,
'Cause we face the judge next week
And I feel like I'm still standing
At the corner of Liberty and State
Waitin for that traffic light to change
From yellow to green.

Michael S. True

The Songwriter

The best of impossible beats in a songwriter's heart
Blessing the tone dead, watering the wall flowers
Anointing the earwig hummers and the shower singers
Bringing us all to that next big digital hit
It is a life lived in perpetual servitude
Trading arpeggios for scattered applause
Crescendos for stroked egos
Assorted tempos for time lost to the muse
Ever the endangered contender
Our musical matador whirls
Dances to pre-dawn hallucinations
Skips across the rocky surface of reality
And chases those ever-elusive symphonic butterflies
All without the aid of baton or metronome
Living the composer's dream,
Musically navigating that endless sea of
Dirty jeans, holy t-shirts, microwavable movements
Aided by the occasional shot of amazing grace
And an ancient tune that seems to be stuck
In the inner recesses of a creative mind
Forever fearful of the dreaded silence
That adrenaline hushing shudder in the dark
This the true troubadour, bleeds to be remembered
Submissively surrendering to the ubiquitous hook
Bowing to the principle of the universal verse
Communing with the power of the cosmic chorus
And ultimately finding religion in the fading resonance
Of that final finished refrain

Michael S. True

More Excuses

Another oil spill…
We stand and watch, all teary eyed
While tanker trucks and rail cars bump and grind,
Super ships cruise from port to port,
Pipelines stretch across the open land;
The thick black sludge sloshing around inside,
Another accident waiting to happen.

We are bad children, pin-pricking a fragile crust.
It is a festering of sores pocked by our obsession,
Abscessed and infected,
We should have let them heal decades ago
But we keep picking at the scabs.

Oh yes, we'll talk of safeguards and contingency plans
While back room bandits subvert safety regulations,
Offer up their band-aid fixes,
But only in the event of some "unforeseen" disaster.

This blatant disregard for worst-case scenarios
Has become our own undoing,
Leaving us with one-too-many all-too-real-life misfortunes:
Toxins tainting tap water,
Chemicals contaminating food,
This crude destroying thousands of fragile ecosystems,
Drilling and fracking
Wrecking our wetlands, our farmlands, our beaches,
Killing off the wildlife and poisoning the people.

All in the name of a cheap lubricant and a fast-buck fuel.

It is not not broken!

So, when will we say, "This folly must come to an end —

True (Cont'd)

This is just wrong — enough's enough?"

For some reason we continue to suck it up.
So too, we continue to make quite the mess.
And, just so you know,
Tears alone won't stop the flow,
Nor will things change with more excuses!

BJ Ward

ODE TO THE MIDDLE FINGER

My first experience
with American sign language.

An international phenomenon:
The English use two fingers
which is really just the middle finger
with his angry buddy—
and how they create a new English
Channel between themselves—

My grandmother was the one
who taught me how to give the finger properly,
Jersey girl that she was.
My father said her finger was the state bird,
spotted up and down the Parkway
throughout the summer.

She sat me on her lap
and said someday the world
will erode me completely,
although it happens slowly—

She said there are agents of the world's acid
that cut one off in traffic
or tell you that unjust wars are justified.

She said to force that acid
through the arm—
let it ball up in a tight fist—

raise that fleshy wrecking ball high above you—

let it become a ship whose cargo is your displeasure,
steered by reprobates,
floating past the edge of your tolerance—

then, my grandmother said, raise the main mast—
hoist the skull and crossbones up it—

As a man now, I have come to realize
how the fingernail was a little polished mirror
she held up to the Medusa world,
hoping to punish it with its own ugliness—

And I wish I could go back to Thanksgiving 1978,
when she first taught me how to give the finger,
to tell her thanks,
and to warn her that the fingerprint
facing her
when she flashed her prolific digit
would one day become a whirlpool
dragging her down
into the world's anger.

That's okay, Grandma would have said.
You'll know yourself one day, my love:
we can't float forever.
On your way down,
sing the world your sign language siren song.
Tell it you know what it's been up to—
bad world, bad world—
and flashing that one finger
shows how you were willing to fight it alone.

Jerry W. Ward, Jr.

White Buffalo in the End: A Prayer

Wakan Tankan, Great Spirit
Our grandmothers, our grandfathers
Unblind us, white lions, us unblind

Let us sing
Mississippi Choctaw blues

Four eyes open, pain, close four ears

In air fire — the body heal
In water earth — the body heal
In fire air — the body heal

Four tongues loosen, peace, four hands enclose

Let us sing
Mississippi Biloxi blues

White crane rides jade turtle
A love supreme
Wakan Tankan
A love supreme
Your master plan

Our grandfathers, our grandmothers
Fill our bowl, bless our rice
White Buffalo. Ashe. White Buffalo.

Wakan Tankan, Great Spirit
A maze of grace in holy space
Thy peace be still when the eagle flies

Let us sing
Mississippi Pascagoula blues

Mike True sings a song he wrote about "a mighty river rolling to the sea."

Two singer songwriters, Claire & Colt Burkett, from the Mississippi coast, delighted the crowd with some original songs. Bottom: Poet Dennis Formento who helped organize the local 100,000 Poets for Change effort.

BJ Ward

"AND ALL THE PEASANTS CHEERED FOR THE KING. THE END."

I close the storybook and my son looks up.
He is swaddled with a bravery he knows nothing about:
      Astronauts floating across his pajamas—
      Soldiers bivouacking on his bookshelf—
      Knights on his lamp—so that his light
          shines right through armor.

"What's a peasant, Daddy?"
I don't think much of the answer: "A poor person."
"Like Grandma and Grandpa?"

And now the story is personal.

My son plays on the junkers my father works on forever—
the front yard is Grandpa's cold scriptoria
and he writes everything in blue collar serifs,
spending his days off rendering metal
into combustion.
Henry Ford invented the printing press
that churned out his Bible.

And my mother with her three shirts that fit—
her Bayonne accent a Cockney in my son's suburban world.

When I lend my parents money, that word has to be used—
lend— or else they wouldn't take it. Even poor people
have Pride as a lawyer.

I was his age when I first knew we were poor.
"Are we poor?" I had asked my mother.
Her eyes were just beginning
their descent deeper into her beauty—
they may have begun

to run away from the world just then,
at her older son's question—

"No," her mouth said, as obviously as possible.

Her hand stroked my hair.
It said, *I'm erasing that question.*

Her tremble said, *Yesterday my boss*
held an empty wallet to my head.

But were we rich somehow?
C'mon—you know the clichés.
But were we rich in another way?

My father knows how to make stillness progress.
At the Foodtown, the cashiers always smiled,
for my mother was an S&H Green Stamp magnate.
My brother and I learned how to love
without dropping our eyes
below the neck.
If money's king, my family served it well.
We only asked to be able to sleep through the night.

And now, my own son is looking up at me,
seeing something he doesn't recognize.
I tell him, "Peasants live in kingdoms,"
and shut out the light—
The astronauts are still fastened in their flotation.
The soldiers still guard the fairytales.

J.E. Warren

GREY - BLUE SKY

In memory of Danny Benefield (1959 - 2016)

The moon is out in a grey-blue sky
I'm all alone on a cold winter night
Your voice rings in my mind
And I can't hide the pain I feel inside

Come my little bird
You've flown so far away
We all wanted you to stay

But they called you away
To a land we don't know
We call it a mystery

That lives in our soul
The love that you've shown
We have all come to know

My dear friend we've traveled till your end
You've taught us more than we can say
The air we breathe, the wind in our sails
Oh, nothing will ever be the same

Dee Warrington

What's In a Kiss?

Remember the Aunt shrunken in her skin?
With shrivelled pursed lips all powdery and downy?
Wanting to salute – hello or goodbye
Then I'd want to shrivel up like her, slinking and shrinking back
Whilst embarrassed elders laughing like tinkling bells
Gush "goodness she's shy…"

Think how prostitutes offer sex,
Bodily contact, bodily fluid each and every
Way for your delight and will use their mouth,
But not for a kiss. Though you could buy one,
Thus turning it away from being a kiss.
Most would refuse as this is real intimacy, a bridge too far.

I circle Rodin's 'The Kiss' the opaque marble
Holding icily the lover's cold kiss
The stolen glance of intimacy
Rodin working it over and over and over in all it's different
Sizes aiming for the perfection of the frozen embrace
Can he carve such deep inference?

The inference of touch, the brush, firm, soft, hard, yielding
Unyielding, romantically, passionately, sexually,
Intimacy shared, leaving memories forever etched
And holding their trace on their lips.
The new lovers fumbling, not quite meeting, roughly,
Earnestly wanting to meet and match.

The kiss a contact between friends and family
Changes when lovers exchange
As when the sea kelp kisses the sea with it's lips
And the tendrils of its hair float as the waves of the water
Wash over it like the swish of a skirt passing by
I remembered you breathing on my lips

As the branches of the tree let their leaves
Kiss the air in the soft breezes as though fabric
Skimmed my body as I dressed.
Enveloping bodies, warm, welcoming like the lovers greeting
Fragrance wafting like a wisp in the sky
What's in a kiss? Everything I miss

Katherine Wyatt

~finding my ass

I found my ass in New Orleans taking a ballet class in Treme. The sun was setting, light streaming through the windows over a dilapidated shotgun home. The light cast my shadow in two dimensions on the studio wall. That's when I found my ass. I had always had a nice ass in my younger years. Ballet is tight assed. Ballet is tight, and anal retentive, and swan-like, and exquisite, but ballet does not HAVE ASS! It was in New Orleans I discovered Samba, slash afro, slash second line dance classes. The teacher, was a tall, statuesque black woman who went to Brazil every year, and taught Samba "Nawlin's style", in Treme on Saturdays. She said it was Brazilian street Samba, but even the white women, the local white women from New Orleans would come to that class, and I would watch in amazement as they danced so quickly, so technically, with round asses that seemed to know Samba the same way I knew grand jetes. New Orleans women don't have to look for their ass, they are naturally in touch with it. It was a white woman in that Samba class that told me to put all of my energy in my ass and wag it. That's when I found my ass. Still, I couldn't shake it like the other ladies. I decided I would try relentlessly anyway. The Samba teacher noticed improvement, and was encouraging, but still came up and hugged me, and said with a laugh, "you are such a ballet dancer".

Eventually Samba came to an end for the winter. After about eight months of trying to master fast footwork, a tight stomach, and an ass that could twitch like popcorn shooting out of a semi-automatic high powered rifle on a hot summer's day. I returned to taking only ballet classes. Whenever my husband and I would go dancing, Samba became a natural way of moving after so much practice. I still wished I could take five pounds off each side of my stomach, and add five to each butt cheek. Women in New Orleans have a special kind of beauty; exotic, strong, independent, and sexual while maintaining enough southern modesty to leaves your imagination to fill in the details. They are ladies, but they have ass.

Wyatt (Cont'd)

As the sun began to set in Treme through the studio window, it caught my shadow on the studio wall, and I noticed a slight increase in the curve of my behind. I smiled, even though it was a ballet class. Genes from my French-Canadian grandmother, were finally winning the battle. As I took first position at the barre, tightened my core, and prepared a port de bras, I knew from my shadow I had started to come in touch with my ass. Round and fuller, like a beignet, the ladies of New Orleans were teaching me how to be a woman of class, while also being able to shake my ass.

George Yatchisin

Do

I love creatures who bob to the earth
with their breathing, whose bodies find life
so much it moves them, whole, each moment.

These creatures also specialize in disappearing,
like the muskrat, now, who retaught me
this lesson, his tender body and slicked hair

suddenly alert to my fidgety watching so that
he can dive under and resume his life
elsewhere, free from my heavy metaphor,

willing merely (and here I underestimate) to be.
Why must it be that certainty is
like the smudge of color I assume is a fish,

holding just below the creek's surface?
I will only know if it moves and I lose it,
as absence becomes answer. And you

sleep upstairs, and I know I would wake you,
if I merely wanted to watch you wear peace
like nothing, like the freckles of your shoulder,

so useless, so beautiful, and rising, not even because
your lungs, doing their thoughtless work, asked them to.
I'm left mistaking everything for the living,

as each stone and blown leaf becomes
whatever I confuse it for, trout and water
snakes, dirt birds and all the things I cannot name.

Top: Poet Rodney Jones is welcomed back to New Orleans by host Nancy Harris (right). Bottom: Poet Terra Durio reads from her new collection, *Last Waters*.

top: Poet Paul Benton reads a poem about balance. Bottom: Poet Steve Beisner reads one of his poems off a smart phone.

Chryss Yost

The Flow

When the water comes, it brings the mountain
and sings the story of the shifting ridge,
summons green to bloom along its edge.
Shapes the hills with patient excavation.

Water comes and carries what we were:
wind-torn leaves, the old path washed away,
the swallowed reflections of hunter and prey.
Brings ash and remains of the bear flag bear.

When water comes, thirst rises for reunion
with the river. All are sullied by the journey.
What blessing to reclaim our purity,
leave the salty stories for the ocean.

We are renewed, to wonder which came first:
that flow of water or this endless thirst?

Caroline Zimmer

Paganini

You are bizarre
as the gnarled tips
of winter's
branches, diddled
by the wind
like little virgin tits.
Pagan prodigy,
since childhood
you lived within
the six strings
of your violin,
six taut veins
to possess our hearts.
Bow string
horse hair
marries
cat gut
and from there
you conjure the creak
of the haunted castle door,
the squealing little girl of yours
her soft stump
imploding
with the thrills
of a man's simian
lust.
Paganini,
gibbous
moon wad,
in the freakish sky,
furtive hell hound,
once, we swooned and sighed.

Once the spellbound pope himself
blessed
your orphic device.
Holy ground
rejects your corpse
for your sorcery's
source,
was Satan's trade —
skillful braid
of notes that made
the soul flinch,
the dead gasp,
the chaste scratch.

Top: Emma Pierson reads a poem about the Mississippi River. Bottom left: Poet Barry Ivker. Bottom right: Poet/photographer Edgar Sierra.

Top left: Katherine Lawrence reads from her collection. Middle: Fatima Shaik reads from her fiction. Bottom: Poet Karel Sloane-Boekbinder with musicians Joy Clark (guitar) and Jenna Vagts (cello).

UNO MFA students pre-sented their poetic works toward the end of their semester. Top left: Jen Hanks. Top right: Jade Hunter. Middle: Heidi McKinley. Bottom: Justin Lamb.

157

Top: Poet Larry Griffin. Bottom left: Elaine Nussbaum. Bottom right: Grace Bauer & Jp Travis.

Top: Poet/fiction writer-
Jimmy Nolan shares
some of his work.
Bottom: Poet Ralph
Adamo.

Poets Rev. Goat Carson & John Sinclair

Poet Dave Brinks & friend on flute.
Below: Writer Dean Paschal and
poet/editor Michael Martin.

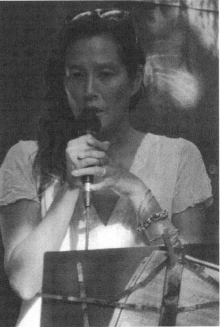

Top left: H.R. Stoneback read from *Singing the Springs* and later played a rousing union song on guitar. Top right: Delia Nakayama read and sang with steel drum accompaniment. Bottom: Professor Arturo Pfister read from his collection of poems titled *My Name is New Orleans*. Next page: Poet Melinda Palacio.

Notes on the Contributors

Ralph Adamo: New Orleans poet, professor and editor; author
 of *Waterblind* and *Ever: Poems 2000--2014* .
Robert Allen: former Marine; pilot; maker of flutes.
Tim Andersen: poet from Chicago
Katy Balma: widely published poet now living in New Orleans;
 former Fulbright scholar.
Grace Bauer: teaches creative writing at Univ of Nebraska; author of
 The Women at the Well and other works.
Steve Beisner: poet & programmer who resides simultaneously
 in Santa Barbara and New Orleans.
Paul Benton: poet; works at WW II Museum; lives in Arabi.
Dave Brinks: author of *The Caveat Onus* and *The Secret Brain.*
Claire & Colt Burkett: songwriters perform as *The Loving Apparitions*.
Megan Burns: host of New Orleans poetry readings at BJs; author of
 Sound and Basin, Commitment; forthcoming: *Basic Progamming.*
Rev. Goat Carson: poet/songwriter, Native American activist.
Maxine Cassin: poet; author of *The Other Side of Sleep.*
Chris Champagne: poet, comic & author of *Roach Opera.*
Dodd Clifton: sailor who sails out of the Delta from Venice, LA.
Marshall Deerfield: (Kavanaugh) traveling poet from NJ/Philly.
Terra Durio: author of *Last Waters.* Lives in Lafayette and N.O.
Scott Edson: poetic storyteller; former actor and mountain climber.
Dean T. Ellis: writer; announcer at WWOZ in New Orleans.
Gina Ferrara: poet; works include *Amber Porch Light* and *Ethereal
 Avalanche.* She also hosts poetry readings at the Latter Library.
Dennis Formento: local poet; author of *Looking For An Out Place.*
Frenchy: artist Randy Frechette. Gallery/studio at 8314 Oak St.
John Gery: teaches creative writing at UNO; author of *Enemies
 of Leisure, A Gallery of Ghosts* and *Have at You Now!*
Mike Goetz: writer, filmmaker, musician. He also pens lyrics for
 a band called Bronze Comet.
Larry Griffin: author of *Cedar Plums*; also a sculptor; lives in OK.
Nancy Harris: longtime host of Maple Leaf Readings and author of
 The Apewoman Story, Mirror Wars and *Beauty Eating Beauty.*
Carolyn Hembree: UNO-based poet; author of *Rigging a Chevy
 to a Time Machine and Other Ways to Escape a Plague.*
Barry Ivker: psychologist & poet; author of *Sonata in F# minor.*
Rodney Jones: prize winning poet has published 11 books of
 poems, including *Things That Happened Once* and *Salvation Blues.*
 Village Prodigies, his new book, will be published in 2017.

Contributors

Julie Kane: former Louisiana state poet laureate; collections include *Jazz Funeral* and *Paper Bullets*. Lives in Natchitoches and Boston.

Maria Melendez Kelson: poetry collections published include *How Long She'll Last in This World* and *Flexible Bones*.

Les Kerr: singer songwriter based in Nashville. His CD recordings include *Contributor, Americana Boogie* and *New Orleans Set*.

Danny Kerwick: N.O./NY poet; author of *Attach It To Earth*, *You Stand Alongside Desire*, and *Behind Lies the Sugar*.

Bill Lavender: poet; publisher of Lavender Ink & Diálogos; author of *Memory Wing*. New poems in chapbook titled *surrealism*.

Katherine Lawrence: Canadian poet; author of *Never Mind* and *Stay*.

Quincey Lehr: poet from NY.

Carolyn Levy: poet, actress; author of *Regina*, a novel set in Uptown New Orleans.

Everette Maddox: one of founders of the Maple Leaf Reading Series; author of *Bar Scotch*, *The Everett Maddox Songbook*, and *American Waste*.

Marjorie Maddox: author of *Local News from Someplace Else*.

Margaret Marley: New Orleans poet and singer.

Mark Marley: retired educator; poet & short story writer.

Michael Martin: editor & author of *Extended Remark: Poems from a Moravian Parking Lot*. Currently resides in North Carolina.

Laura Mattingly: poet & activist; author of *The Book of Incorporation*.

Charlotte Mears: her collections of poems include *Sweet Air*.

Robert Menuet: poet & educator.

Michael "Quess?" Moore: poet & educator; author of *Blind Visionz* and *Sleeper Cell*.

Geoff Munsterman: poet & publisher; graduate of NOCCA; author of *Because the Stars Shine Through It*.

Kay Murphy: author of *Belief Blues, Autopsy* and other collections; poetry prize named in her honor at the University of New Orleans.

Delia Nakayama: teacher and lively practioner of poetry.

Jimmy Nolan: short story writer & novelist; titles include *Higher Ground* and *Perpetual Care*.

Elaine Nussbaum: visiting poet/writer. Often lives in Oregon.

Biljana Obradovic: poet, university professor & translator; author of *Frozen Embraces* and *Little Disruptions*.

Nina Ouedraogo: poet & researcher; originally from Africa

Melinda Palacio: bi-lingual poet & novelist; works include *How Fire Is A Story, Waiting* and *Ocotillo Dreams*.

Contributors (Cont'd)

Dean Paschal: short story writer/novelist; author of *By the Light of the Jukebox*; recent published story in *The Uncanny Reader* anthology.

Ingid Pavia: writer with roots in New Orleans & Idaho.

Spike Perkins: New Orleans-based musician, poet, short story writer.

Valentine Pierce: poet & designer; author of *Geometry of the Heart*

Emma Pierson: poet & educator. She has a forthcoming collection of poems about her love affair with New Orleans.

Paul Pines: NY-based poet & psychotherapist; author of *Last Call at the Tin Palace*, *Divine Madness*, and several other works.

Arthur Pfister: prolific poet & educator; author of *My Name is New Orleans*, *Jazz Stories*, and *A Love Supreme.*

Manfred Pollard: New Orleans-based poet, musician & painter.

James M. Robinson: author of *Boca del Rio* & *The Caterpillars of St. Bernard.*

Jimmy Ross: storyteller poet; author of *Say What?*

David Rowe: poet & social worker; author of *Unsolicited Poems*.

Vicki Salloum: writes fiction; novels include *A Prayer to Saint Jude* and *Faulkner and Friends.*

Fatima Shaik: author of *What Went Missing and What Got Found.*

Edgar Sierra: bi-lingual poet; photographer; originally from Columbia.

John Sinclair: poet, singer songwriter & radio personality.

Karel Sloane-Boekbinder: poet, singer; involved in haiku society.

C.M. Soto: writer, playwright, screenwriter. Author of *These are the Rooms to my Mother's House* (Ice Scream Theater). She also performs as Vinylux at various venues and events.

Sulla: (aka Charles Morgan) has written several chapbooks.

H.R. Stoneback: NY-based poet, professor & musician; author of *Singing the Springs, Cafe Millennium* and other collections.

Paris Hughes Tate: graduate of NOCCA in poetics; works as a librarian in New Orleans.

Lucy Tierney: writer; lives on the northshore of Lake Pontchatrain.

JP Travis: writer; works include *Pitching in the Dark* & *JJ's Journal.*

Michael S. True: singer songwriter, poet, painter, musician; author of *Diabolical Seas* and several CDs of his own original songs.

BJ Ward: poet & educator; collections include *Gravedigger's Blrthday* and *Jackleg Opera*; has been featured on NPR; lives in New Jersey.

Jerry W. Ward, Jr.: poet & educator; author of *The Katrina Papers: A Book of Trauma and Recovery* and co-author of *The Cambridge History of African American Literature.*

Contributors (Cont'd)

Jonathan Warren: poet/musician; author of *Go to the River*.
Dee Warrington: poet who usually resides in London, England.
Katherine Wyatt: poet & former professional dancer.
George Yatchisin: California-based poet.
Chryss Yost: California-based poet; author of *Mouth and Fruit*.
Caroline Zimmer: poet was raised on Bourbon St.; graduate of
    NOCCA in creative writing; lives in French Quarter, tends bar.

***